THINKING LIKE A SCIENTIST

♡ LIKED THE BOOK? A REVIEW ON AMAZON MEANS THE WORLD TO US.

2023 Noah Press © All Rights Reserved

All rights reserved. No part of this publication may be reproduced, distributed, or transmitted in any form or by any means, including photocopying, recording, or other electronic or mechanical methods, without the prior written permission of the publisher, except in the case of brief quotations embodied in critical reviews and certain other noncommercial uses permitted by copyright law.

This book is a biography. Information contained within this book is for educational purposes only. Although the author and publisher have made every effort to ensure that the information in this book was correct at press time, the author and publisher do not assume and hereby disclaim any liability to any party for any loss, damage, or disruption caused by errors or omissions, whether such errors or omissions result from negligence, accident, or any other cause.

TALK TO US

hello@noah-press.com

dedicated to every child out there - **you can be anything you want to be**.

Sophia jumped up and down excitedly. She couldn't wait to try out her new telescope! She had waited all day to look at the stars. Finally, the sun went down, down, down behind the big hill on the horizon. It was time!

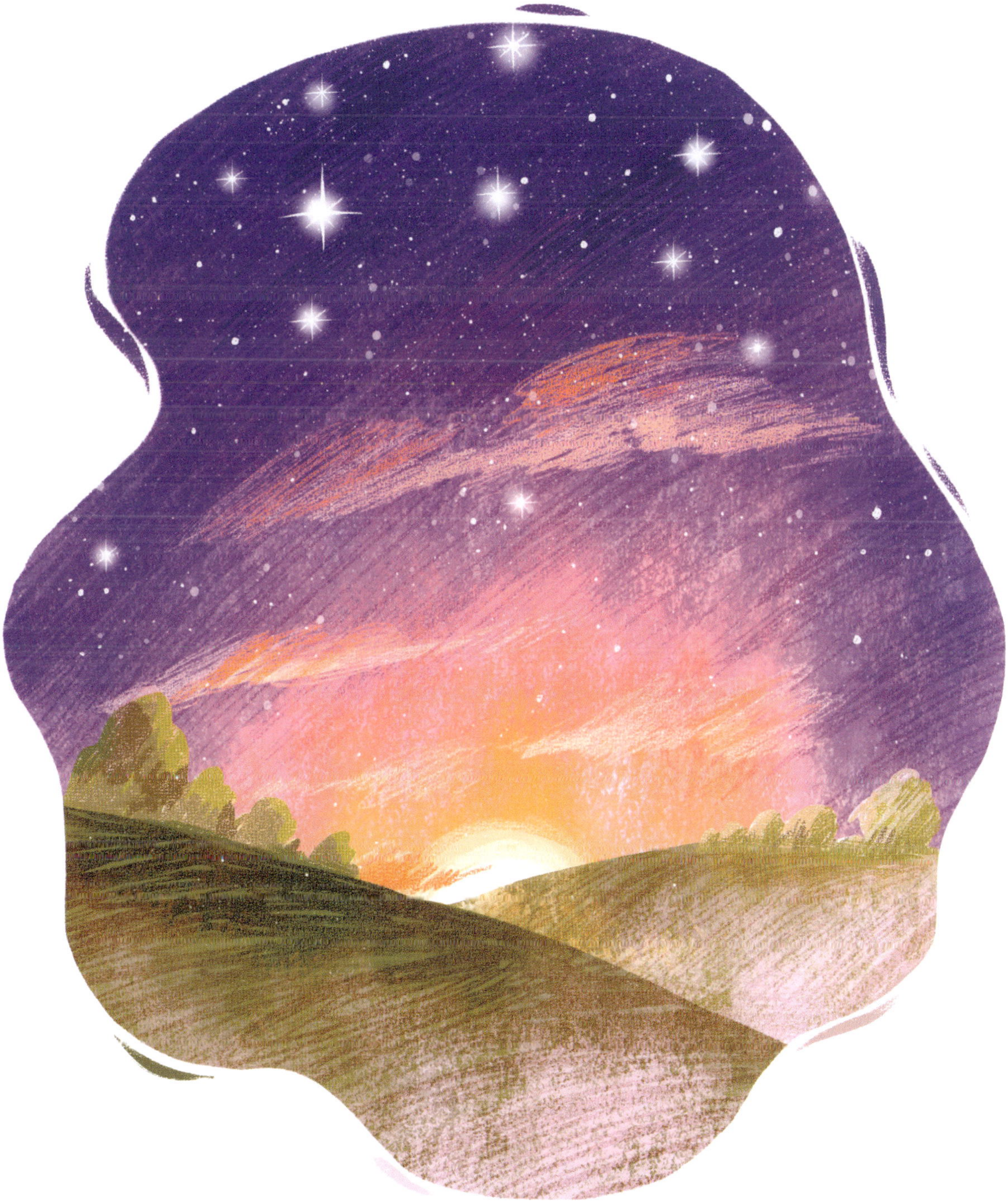

Her telescope was already set up at her bedroom window, pointing to the night sky. Sophia put her eye to the lens and turned the dial slowly until a shining star was brought into focus.

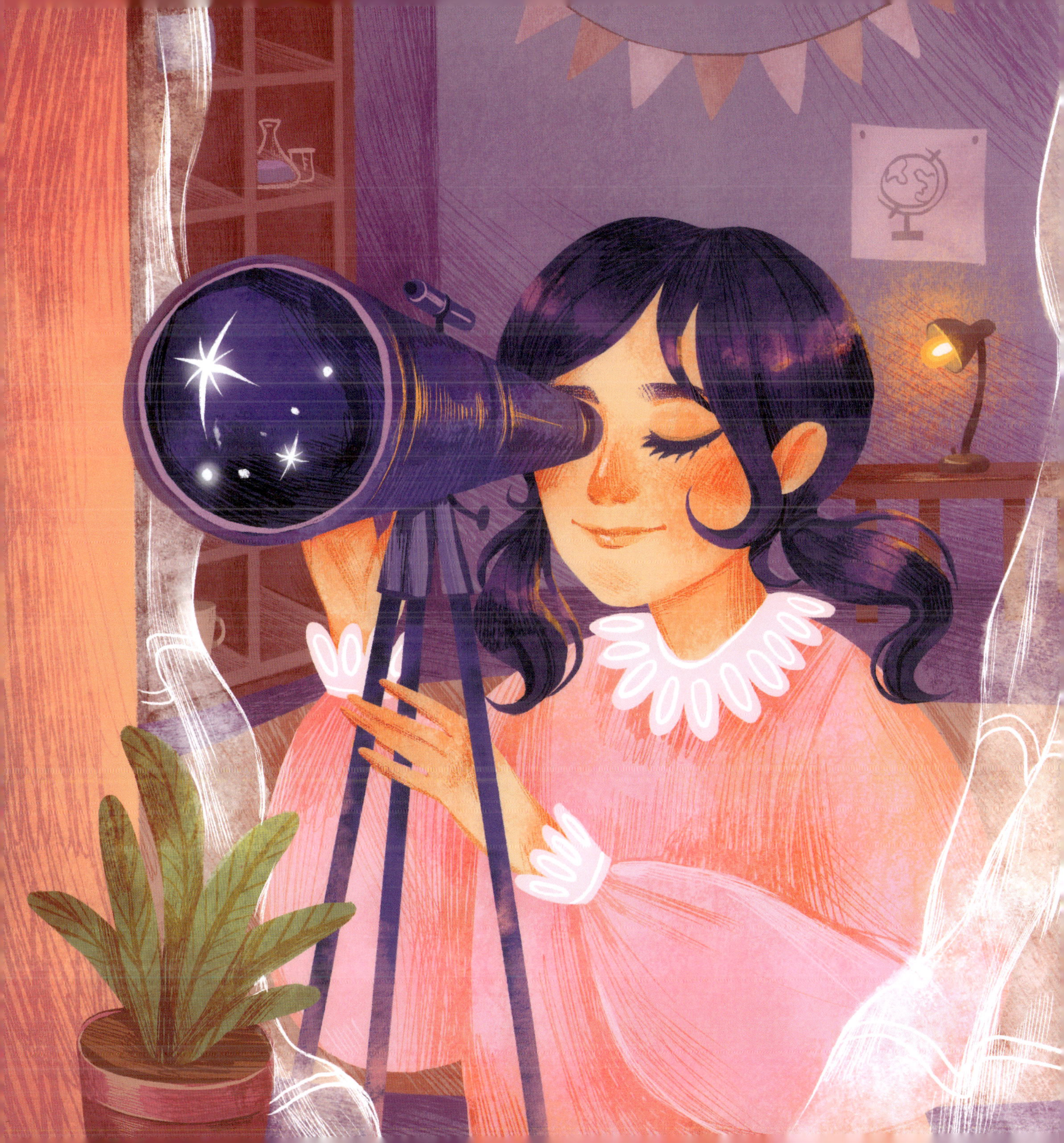

As she slowly moved the telescope from left to right, she was amazed at how many stars there were. She tried to count them, but it was impossible!

Suddenly, a small light caught her eye. It wasn't "twinkly" like a star, but instead, it was a tiny, solid light moving quickly across the sky.
"Do stars move?" Sophia whispered to herself.
"I've never seen a star like this before. In fact, I don't think it's a star at all!"

As she'd been taught by her Science teacher, Mr. Newton, Sophia came up with a hypothesis. Now, in case you don't know what a hypothesis is, it's an educated guess about something you're trying to figure out.

Sophia had observed that the small light in the sky was different than the stars. Because it was moving across the sky in one steady direction, her hypothesis was: The object is not a star, but something else in the solar system.

Quickly, Sophia turned on the lamp and grabbed her science book about astronomy. Oh, how she loved books about the universe! She flipped the pages until she found a chapter titled, How Satellites Are Different Than Stars.

"Ah-ha!" Sophia exclaimed. "The light that is moving across the sky is a satellite. They look like tiny stars, but they are actually man-made machines that orbit the earth."

She looked through her telescope again and saw that the satellite had moved quite a distance! Her conclusion was right, and her scientific research was a success!

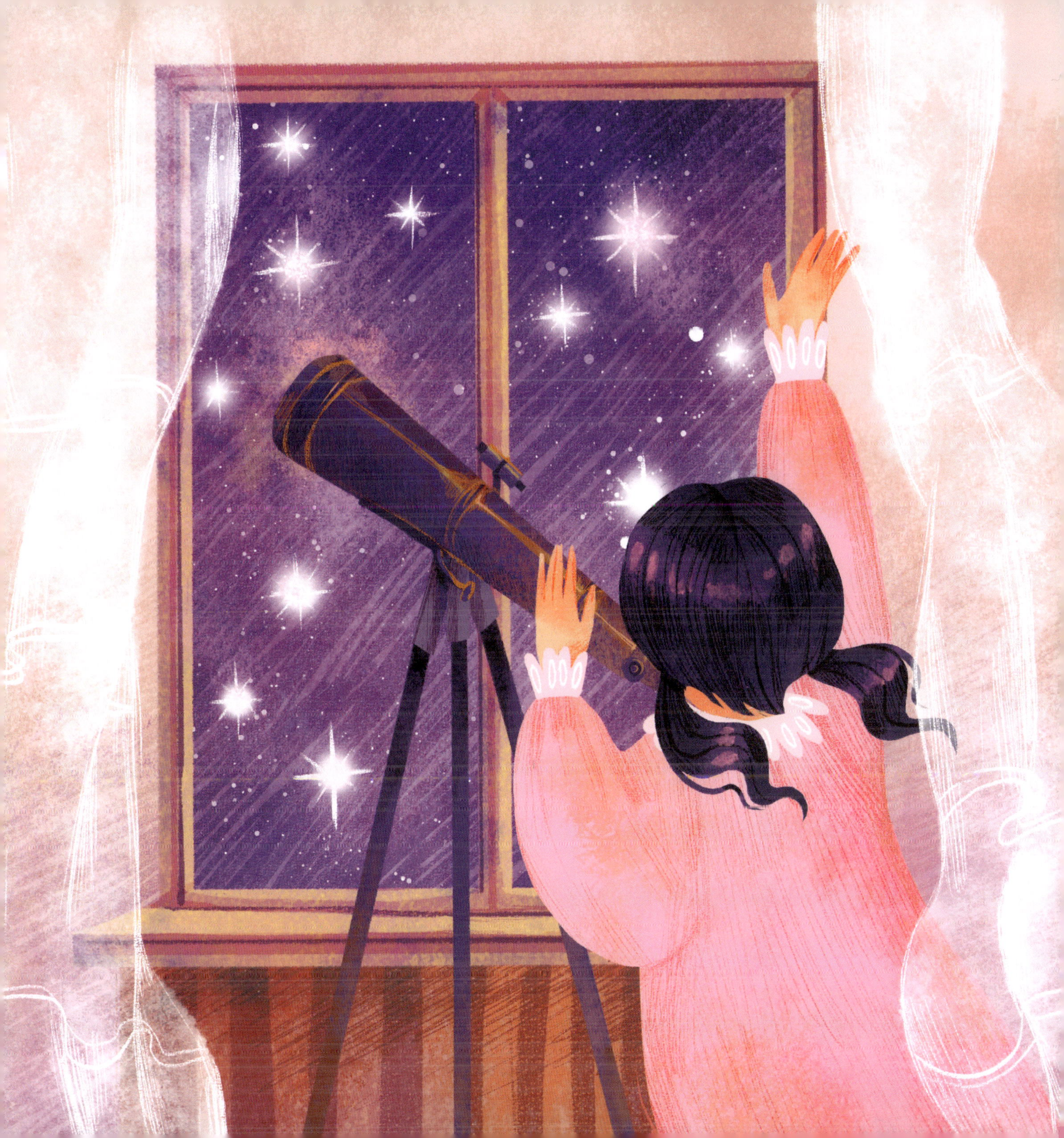

The next day at school, Sophia was playing on the playground with her friends. She was going down the slide when she noticed Liam and Michael on the swings.

Liam was moving his legs back and forth, swinging high in the sky. Michael, on the other hand, was moving his legs back and forth, but not swinging high at all.

Hmm... Sophia thought. I wonder why Liam is swinging so much higher than Michael. There must be a scientific explanation! She went to sit under a big shade tree to observe them and make notes about what she observed.

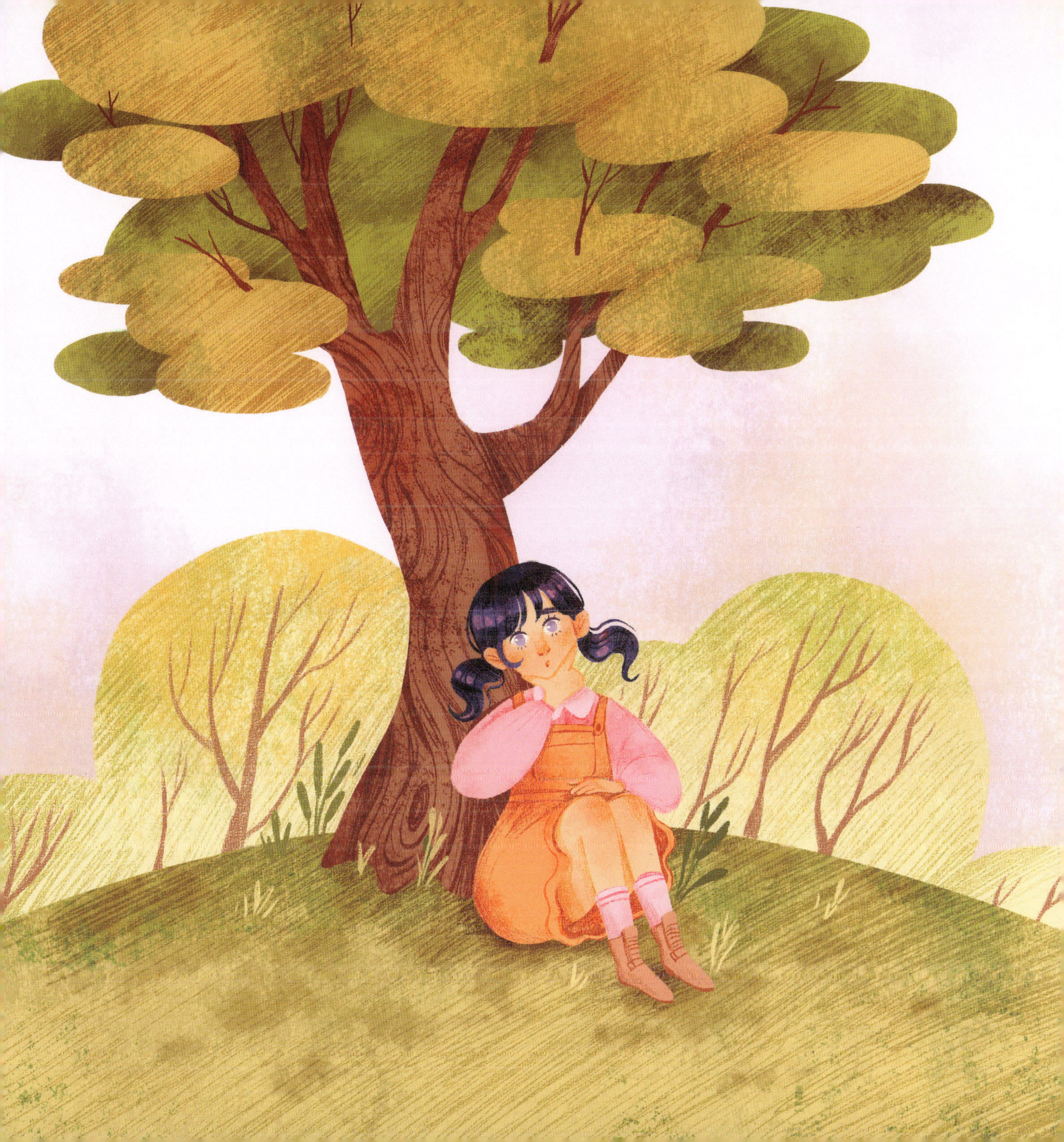

Taking out a notebook and pencil from her backpack, Sophia wrote down the similarities and differences between Liam and Michael.

1. Both Liam and Michael were about the same height and weight.
2. Both swings were the same size and the same distance from the ground.
3. Liam was moving his legs back and forth quickly, while Michael wasmoving his legs slowly.

"That must be it!" Sophia said aloud. She remembered the science unit about physics, and how potential energy and kinetic energy work together.

Her hypothesis was: Liam is swinging higher because he is building up more potential energy. Michael is swinging lower because he is using less potential energy. The longer she watched the boys on the swings, the more her hypothesis was proved right!
Liam produced more kinetic energy by kicking his legs rapidly. Michael produced less kinetic energy by moving his legs slowly.

Sophia wrote the conclusion in her notebook and put it in her backpack. She loved thinking like a scientist!

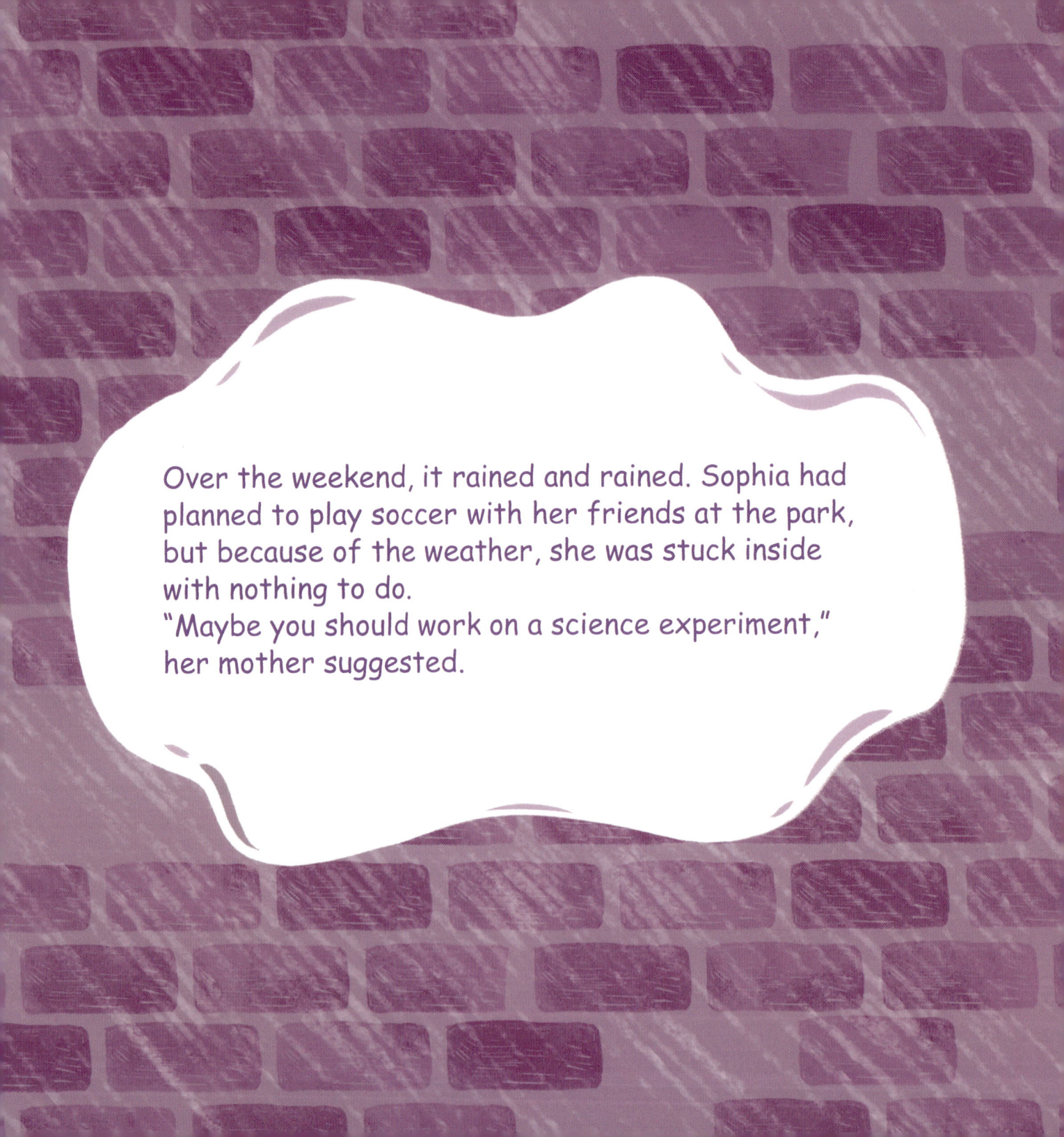

Over the weekend, it rained and rained. Sophia had planned to play soccer with her friends at the park, but because of the weather, she was stuck inside with nothing to do.
"Maybe you should work on a science experiment," her mother suggested.

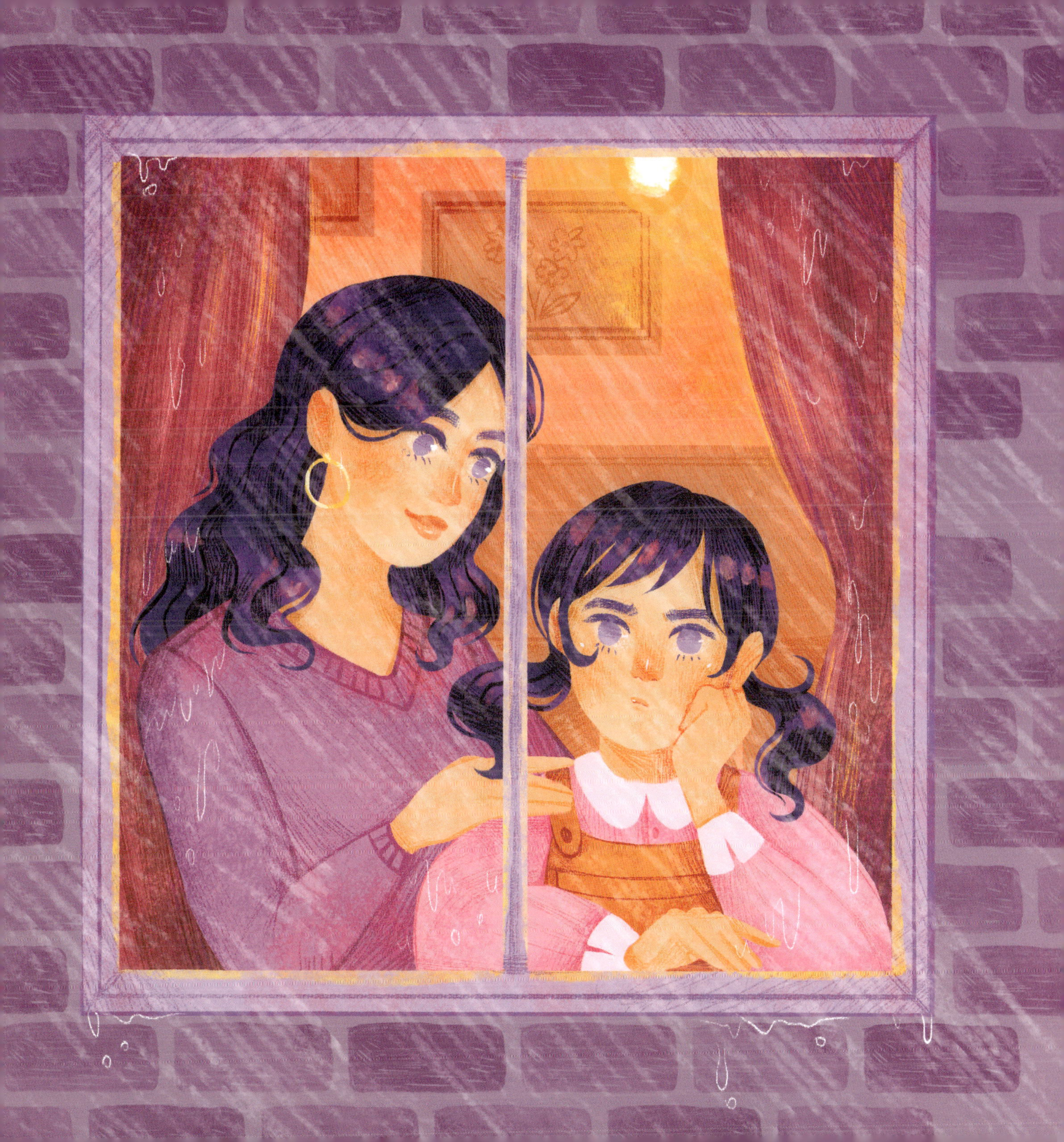

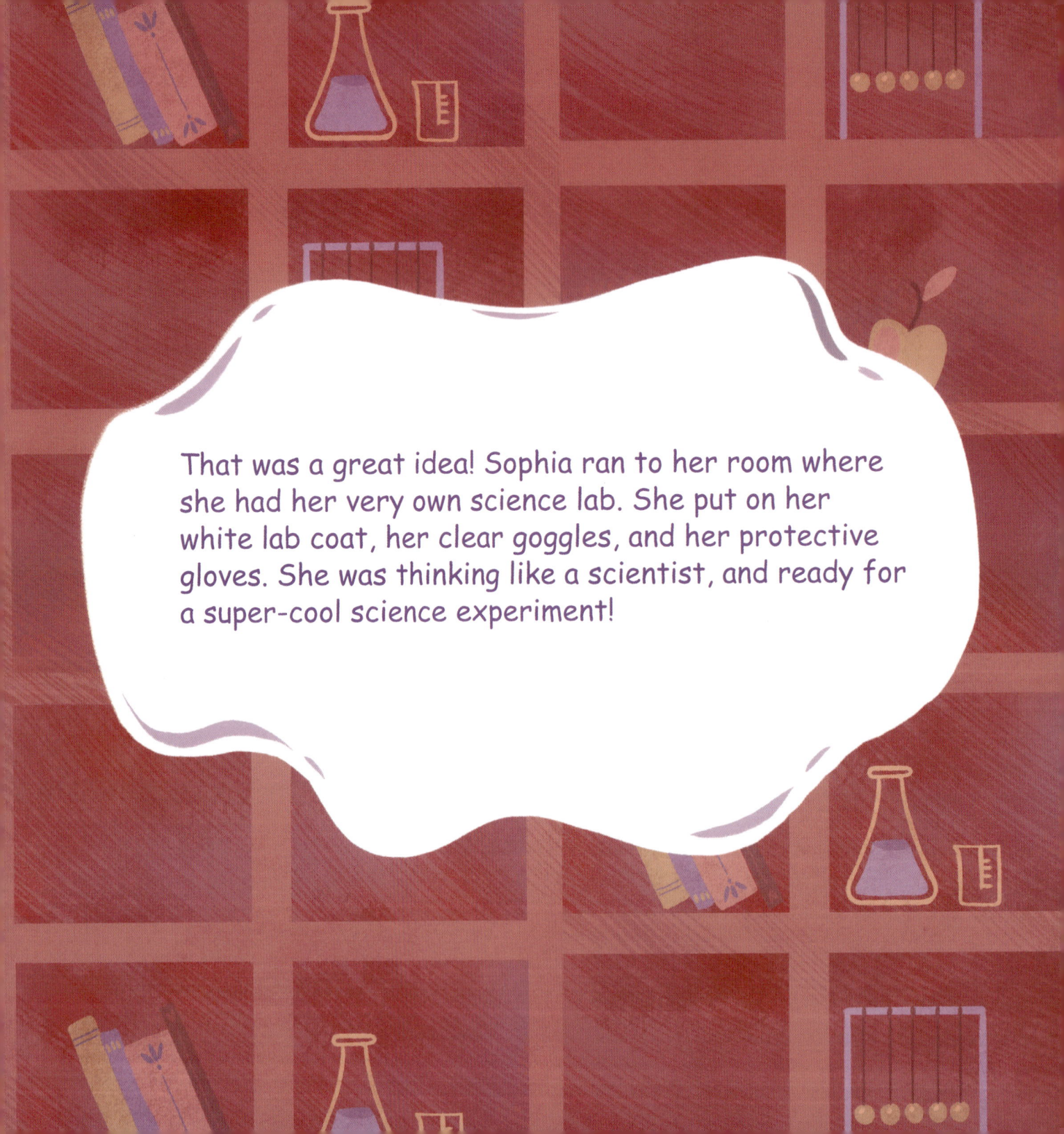

That was a great idea! Sophia ran to her room where she had her very own science lab. She put on her white lab coat, her clear goggles, and her protective gloves. She was thinking like a scientist, and ready for a super-cool science experiment!

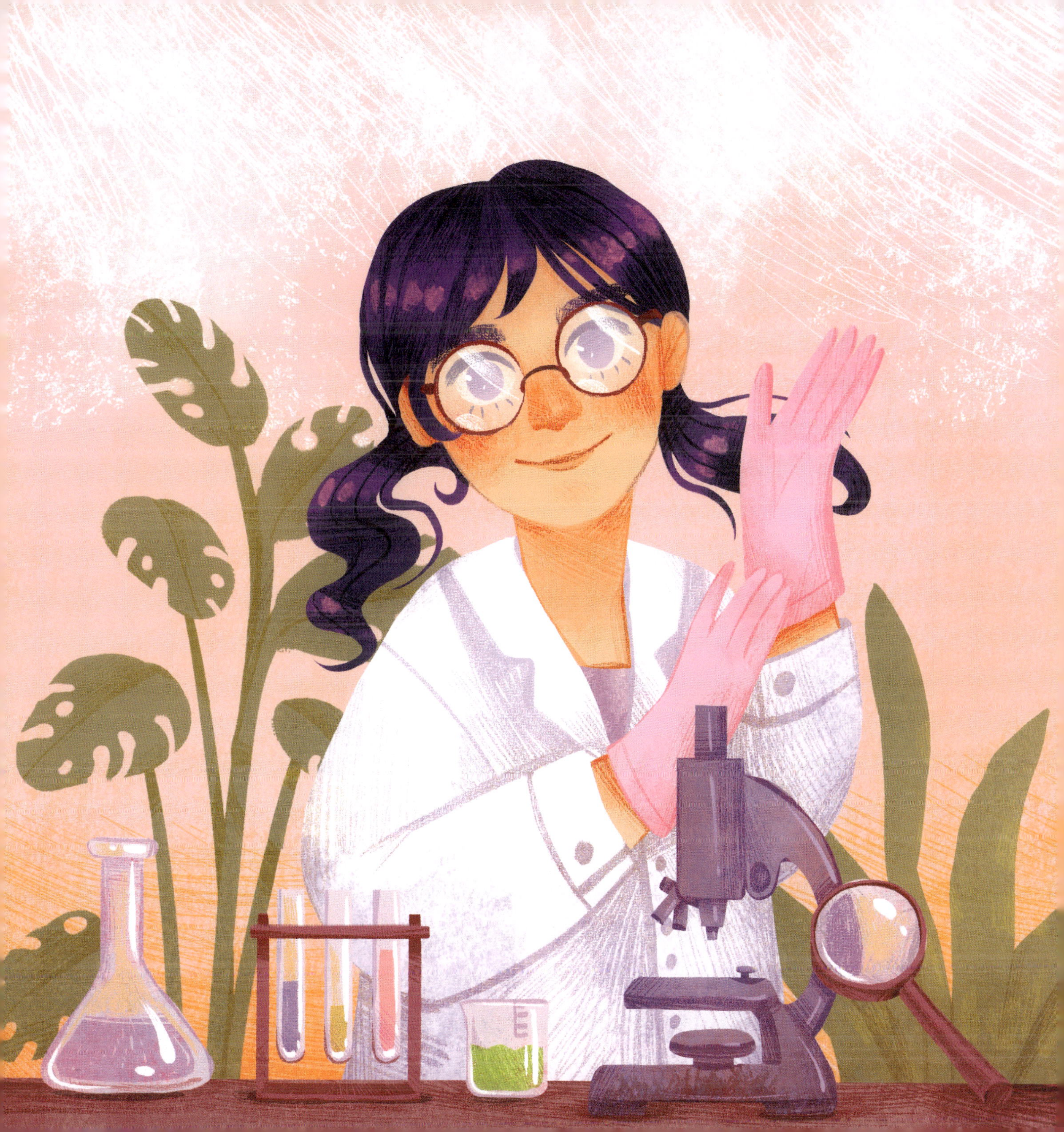

Looking out the window, Sophia observed the big, dark clouds looming overhead. She wondered why some clouds float across the sky on sunny days, while other clouds produce rain on stormy days.

Her hypothesis was: The clouds that produce rain are filled with so much moisture, they can't hold it in.

Turning to her science experiment, she filled a glass with water and squirted a layer of shaving cream on top. Then, she sprinkled drops of food coloring on top of the shaving cream.

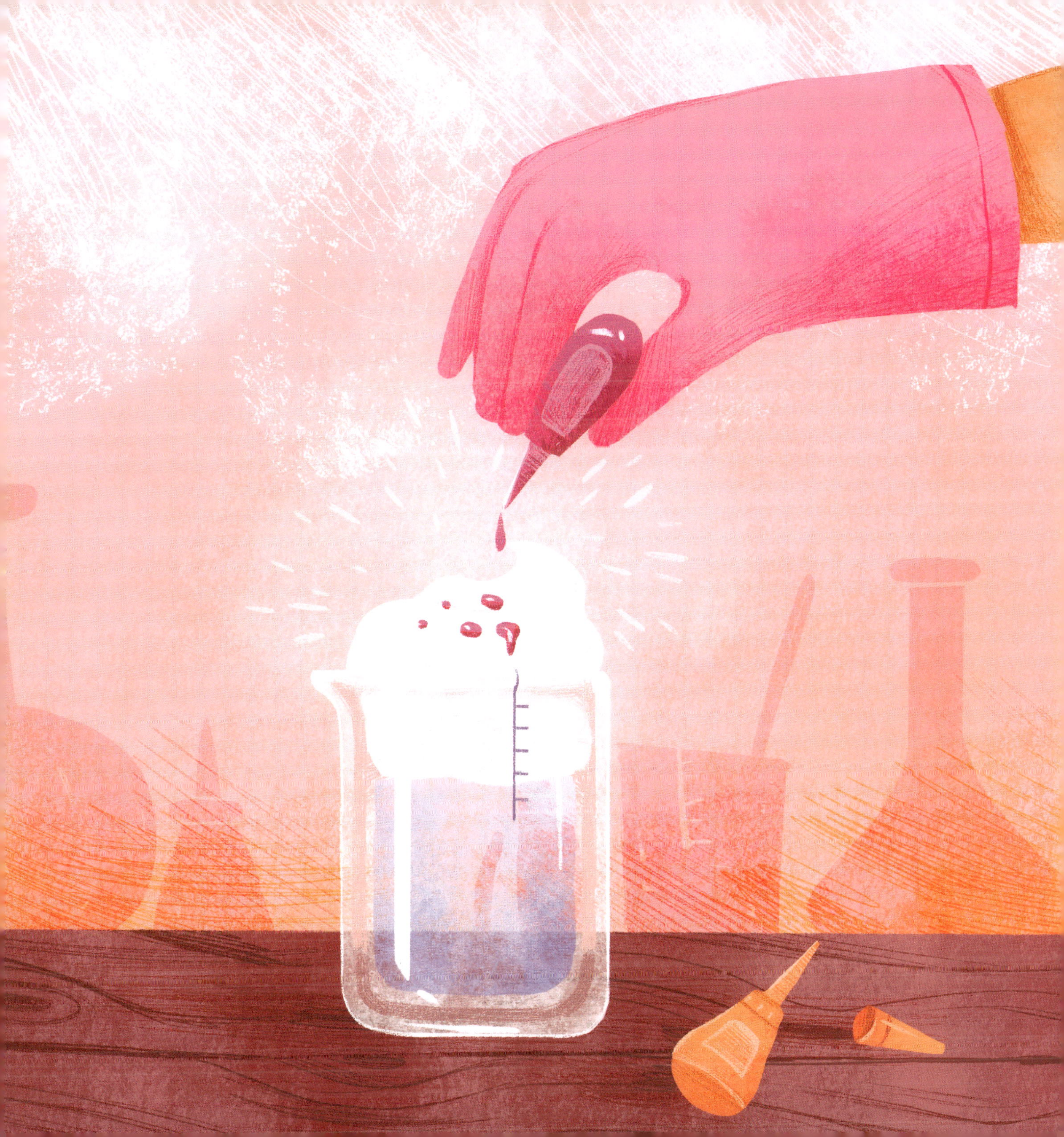

Using her magnifying glass, Sophia watched as the drops of food coloring began to fall into the water below. Drop, drop, drop...just like rain!

She concluded that the cloud of shaving cream could not hold all of the food coloring. Eventually, gravity pulled the moisture down into the glass, forming colorful raindrops.

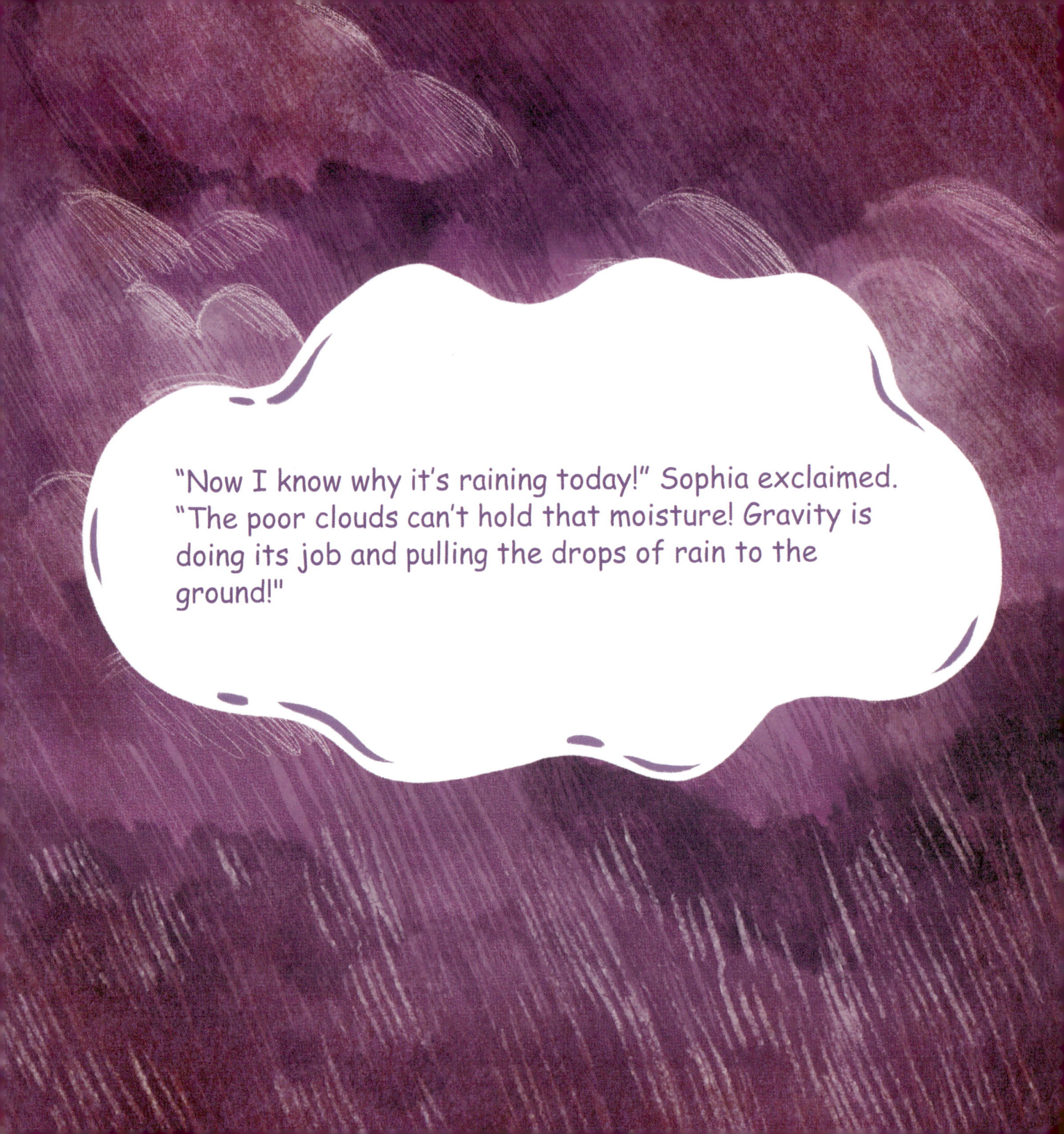

"Now I know why it's raining today!" Sophia exclaimed. "The poor clouds can't hold that moisture! Gravity is doing its job and pulling the drops of rain to the ground!"

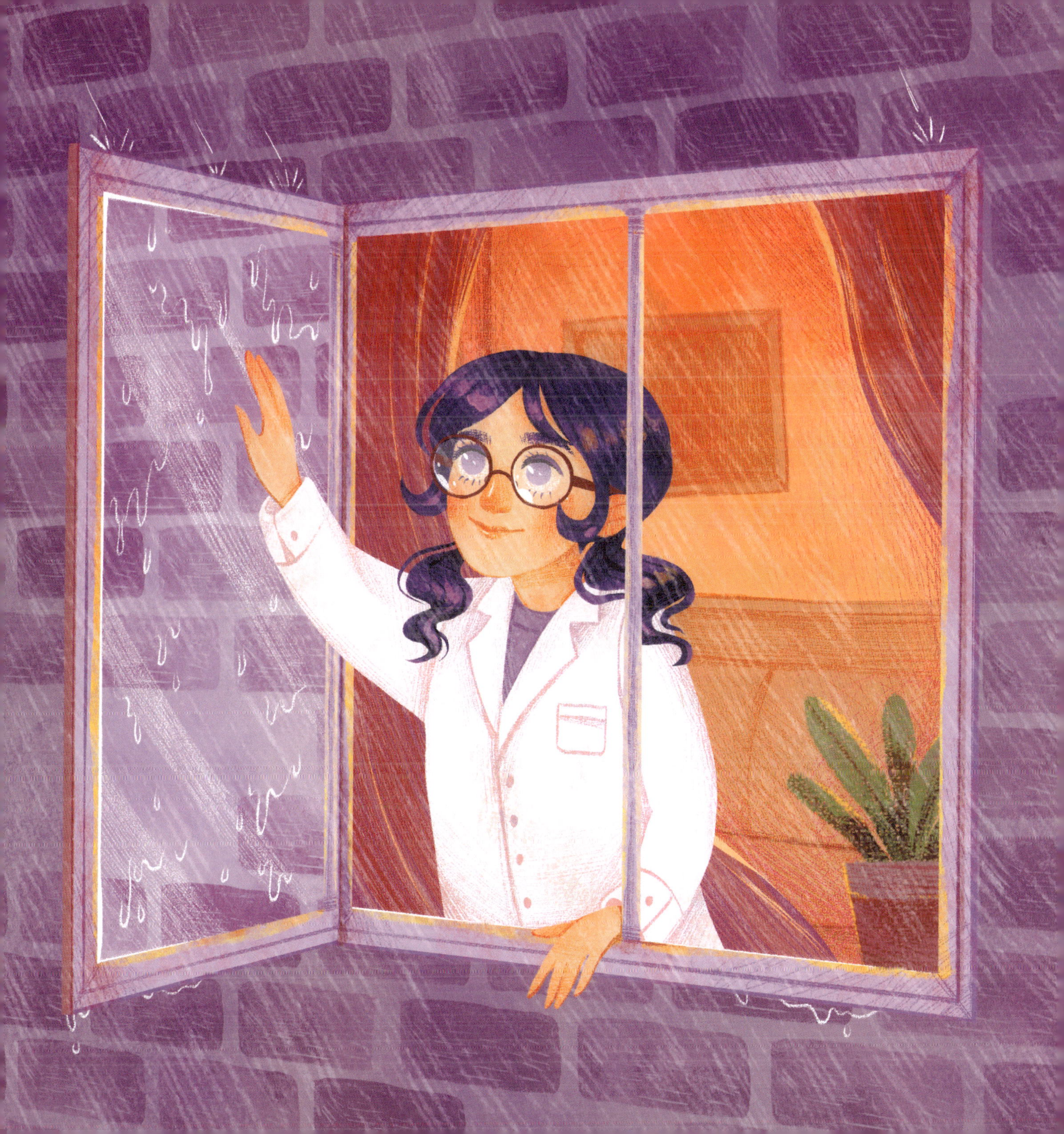

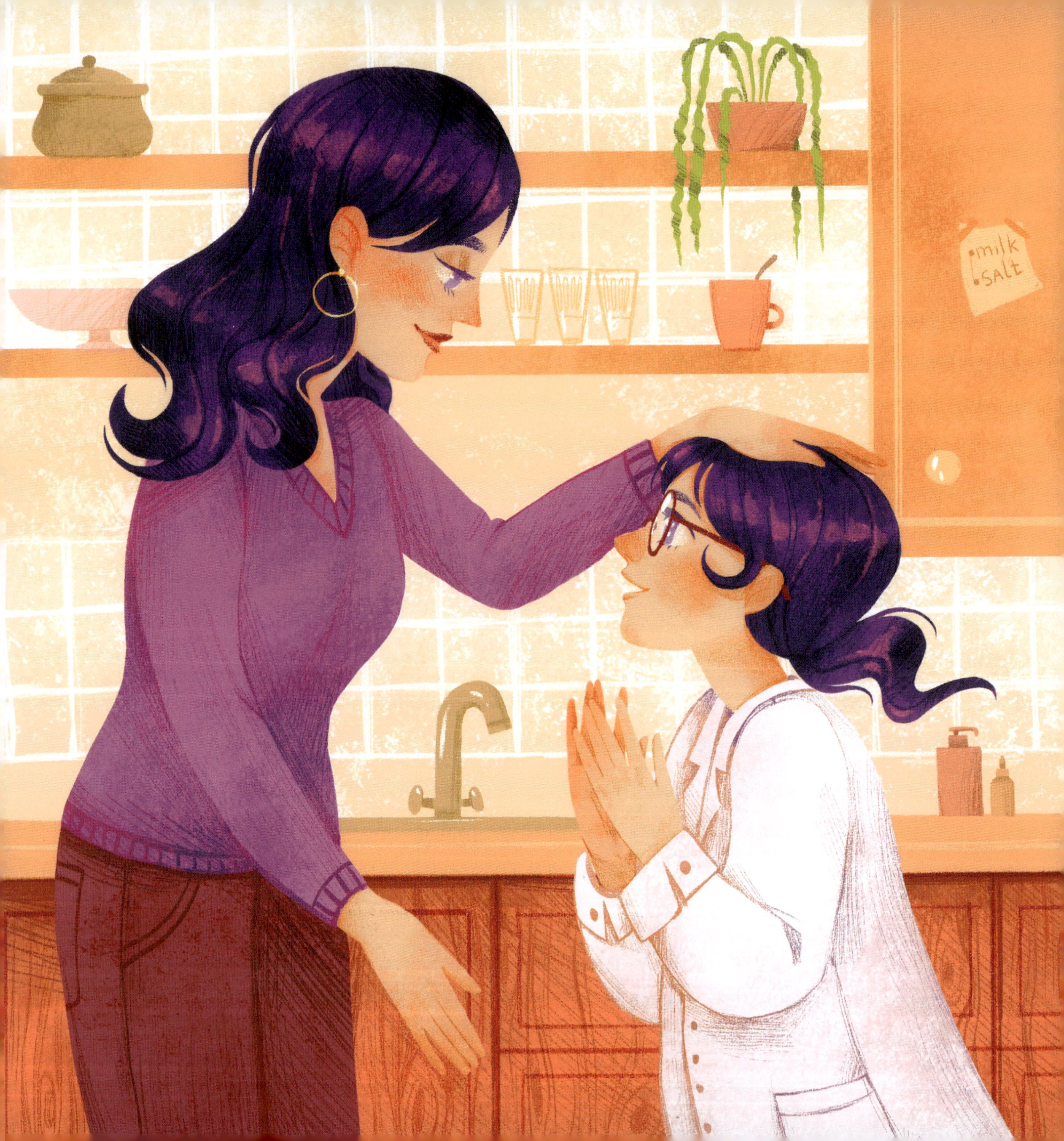
milk
salt

Sophia ran to tell her mom all about her experiment. "That sounds fun!" her mother said. "You think just like a scientist, my girl. Perhaps, you'll grow up to make many more scientific discoveries!"

Sophia beamed proudly. She loved thinking like a scientist, and she couldn't wait to explore more of the big, wide world around her.

So, what about you? Do you enjoy thinking like a scientist? I can't wait to see what amazing things you'll discover!

Printed in Great Britain
by Amazon